MW01490494

STOP ACTING LIKE A GIRL

A GUIDE TO OVERCOMING THE NORMS THAT HOLD WOMEN BACK

STACEE SANTI LONGFELLOW

FOX FORCE FIVE PUBLISHING

ISBN 979-8-9915249-0-2
Library of Congress Control Number 2024921695
1st edition October 2o24
Published and distributed by Fox Force Five Publishing, LLC,
PO Box 776, Bayfield, Colorado, 81122

CONTENTS

For my nieces, Lindsay and Elizabeth, as you embark on your own incredible journeys—may you always believe in your strength and potential.

And to my parents, whose unwavering belief in me taught me that I can achieve anything, regardless of my gender.

And perhaps
What made her beautiful
Was not her appearance
Or what she achieved,
But in her love
And in her courage
And her audacity
To believe
No matter
The darkness
Around her.
Light ran wild
Within her,
And that was the way
She came alive
And it showed up
In everything.

—Morgan Harper Nichols

A NOTE FROM THE AUTHOR

The content in this book comes from my own experiences and insights into the challenges as a traditional girl and woman in the workplace. My goal is to highlight common habits and mindsets formed during childhood that can unintentionally hold women back in their professional lives.

That said, I want to emphasize that I recognize the diversity of gender identities. While this book is specifically geared toward those who identify as traditional girls and women, the tips and strategies shared can help anyone navigate the complex professional world. I hope this book empowers readers to feel supported, thrive in their careers, and go after their dreams regardless of gender. If it resonates with you, it's all yours!

UNLEARNING THE "GIRL RULES"

Picture this: I'm five years into running my tech startup, and the pressure is on. Competition is fierce, and I finally have enough money to hire a VP of Sales—someone who can take my mobile app company to the next level. I put out a call on LinkedIn, sift through dozens of resumes, conduct multiple interviews, and find the perfect candidate. But unlike the other hires, this guy was a tough negotiator. I lay out the financial situation and explain exactly what I can afford. He listens and then says, "That's all fine, but if you want me on your team, this (X) is what I need."

Around the same time, I was conducting annual performance reviews for my all-women team. One by one, I asked them what they wanted for a raise. Almost every response was the same: "Whatever you think is possible." Now, these weren't just any employees—they were an exceptional group of women who had stuck with me through the ups and downs of startup life. Each brought something unique to the table, shining in their own way. Curious, I tried something different. I told them to go home, think it over, and come back the next day with a request as if they were negotiating like a man. And guess what? Every single one returned with a more assertive and specific demand.

That's when it hit me. Why hadn't these women negotiated with me the way the new-hire man did? Were they more concerned about the company's well-being than their own? Maybe. Were they simply being polite? Probably. But was this mindset holding them back? Absolutely.

For years, I had worked predominantly with women—through veterinary school and two decades of practice in a field that's over 80% female. I thought I knew how women operated, what motivated them, and how to communicate with them effectively. But starting my tech company opened my eyes. When it came to the big deals—the corporate contracts, distribution agreements, investor meetings, and eventual acquisitions—the decision-makers in the room were

80% men. So where were all the women? I started paying close attention to the 10-20% of women in leadership roles, observing how they made decisions, talked about money, shared their opinions, and held their ground in a room. What I noticed was that they approached things differently than most women—they weren't playing by the usual "girl rules."

The realization wasn't just about my team—it was about the broader truth that too many women face. From a young age, we're taught to be agreeable, to play nice, and not to disrupt the status quo. But in business, especially in leadership, that mindset can be a serious disadvantage. The women on my team were just as capable as the man I hired, but their conditioning held them back from asking for what they truly deserved. That moment became a turning point for me and the driving force behind this book.

It's time to stop acting like "girls" and start embracing the assertiveness, confidence, and unapologetic ambition that men often display without hesitation. This isn't just about negotiating for a raise or a promotion; it's about unlearning the norms that have held us back for too long and stepping into the power that's rightfully ours. In the chapters ahead, we'll dig into how to break free from these limiting expectations and embrace the behaviors that will propel us forward to be more like the women in the boardrooms.

As you dive into this book, the first skill to sharpen is your judgment. Take what resonates with you and your unique situation. If some tips don't align with your style, don't work for you, or bring too much pushback, let them go. These strategies worked for me in my journey, but that doesn't mean they're a perfect fit for everyone. Trust yourself to decide what's relevant and leave the rest behind.

Last but not least, I want to be clear: Not all women fall into these patterns, and not all men avoid them. In fact, I know a few guys who are worse at these habits than all my female friends combined. But I'm speaking from my experience as a woman who had to navigate a male-dominated C-suite, so that's the perspective you'll find here.

"I did everything he did but backwards and in high heels."

— Ginger Rogers

BE DECISIVE

Letting go of the "girl" mindset is just the start. The first game-changer is embracing decisiveness—a key trait that separates successful women leaders from the rest of the pack.

Being decisive is about showing the world that you know what you want. Too often, girls are taught that it's polite to let others take the lead, to go with the flow. But when you consistently defer to others, people start to see you as a follower, not a leader. And here's the thing—decisiveness isn't just about the big, life-changing decisions. It's about owning your choices in the everyday moments, whether it's picking out your outfit, choosing the movie for date night, or deciding where to go for lunch.

Picture this: You're at work, and it's time to order pizza for lunch. Instead of shrugging and saying, *"I don't care, whatever you all want"*—which, let's be honest, isn't true—take the wheel. Say, *"I'm feeling pepperoni with black olives and tomatoes on thin crust."* It's not just about pizza; it's about showing that you have a voice and aren't afraid to use it.

Especially when you're still figuring out who you are and where you fit in, it's crucial not to get labeled as the indecisive one. Making decisions, even on something as small as pizza toppings, helps you define your identity and lets others know that you're confident in your choices.

> *Each time you voice your opinion, you're flexing that decision-making muscle and saying, "Hey, this is me, and I'm here to make my mark."*

Consistently making good decisions is a cornerstone of leadership. And while deciding what to wear or what to eat might seem simple, it's this practice on the small stuff that prepares you for the big stuff—like whether to quit your job or let an employee go.

Mastering Big Decision-Making

So, how do you make good decisions? Here are seven tips that helped me:

1. List your priorities. When it comes to making a decision, it's helpful to think about your priorities and goals for the matter at hand. We often get derailed and lose sight of the original reason we set out to do something. When you have clarity on the "why" you are doing something, it will help you determine the "how."

2. Gather information. You need to know the facts of the potential choices on the table.

I like to ask myself these questions:

- How hard is it going to be? (logistics, effort, knowledge needed)
- How long is it going to take? (hours, weeks, months, years)
- How expensive is it going to be? (I have the money vs. I will have to get a loan)

Let's say, for example, you are trying to decide whether or not to go to college after high school. It's quite possible, and normal I might add, to not have any idea what you want to do with the rest of your life at this particular moment. So, here are a few questions to ponder when you are deciding if college is right for you:

- How hard is it going to be?
- Do you mind learning new things?
- How do you feel about moving away from home?
- How long of a commitment will it be? Two years? Four years?
- How much money will it cost?
- Will you, or your parents, be in debt?
- How long will it take to pay it back?
- Will you be able to get a better job than if you don't have a college education?

There are a couple of traps to be aware of when gathering information. The first trap is being overly attached to your point of view, which causes you to be so biased that you can't equally consider other outcomes. The second trap is analysis paralysis, where you put off making a decision until you have a clear-cut path laid out in front of you. Having a clear-cut path laid out in front of you rarely happens. If it were an easy or obvious decision, you would have already made it.

Making a decision usually requires you to accept a level of uncertainty and discomfort.

3. Play out the best-case scenario for each of the choices.

Think about what success in each decision looks like. Try to picture the best outcome in your mind. Ask yourself *"Then what?"* and repeat that at least three times. This may play out something like this:

If I take the new job as VP and I crush it, then what? Then I can advance to Senior VP, and then what? Then I can advance to CEO, and then what? Then I will be working 50 to 60 hours a week, and I'll have to move to HQ in the city. I will be leading boardroom meetings, budgets, and the company trajectory. Then picture yourself in this life and focus on how that feels. Is this the life you dream about?

For me, it was veterinary school. Yes, it would be four more years of college. Yes, I would go into serious debt. Yes, I would be able to get a job I loved. The idea of taking care of animals every day, doing surgery, and working in a busy practice was everything I dreamed about. I couldn't imagine doing anything else. That's when I knew I was on the right track.

If you are going to put your heart and soul into your goal, then knowing where the road to success leads is essential.

4. Play out the worst-case scenario for each of the choices.
Let's face it, life is tough. Things rarely go as planned, so understanding the risks of each choice on the list is critical. The idea here is to be aware of the real possibility of what you might face if things don't go as planned.

When I was trying to decide if I should quit my six-figure corporate job to start my own company, it was a real possibility that I would have to downgrade my lifestyle. Was I prepared to downgrade my house, my car, and my Starbucks addiction if needed? How did my husband feel about this? What if my new business failed, then what? I would have to try to get my old job back and perhaps start at a lower position with the company. Could I live with this? There is no right or wrong answer, but failing to play out the worst-case scenario makes it hard to make a good decision.

5. Seek input. It's often hard to see the forest for the trees, so reaching out to a couple of trusted advisors is never a bad idea. Seek out individuals who you respect and who have your best interests at heart. These may be friends, colleagues, mentors, or family members. Share your priorities and talk through your options with them. They may offer a different perspective that helps you think about your choices in a new light.

When I was trying to decide if I should sell the company I loved so much for life-changing money, my mother said, *"I am sure you have more ideas in your head if you ever wanted to start another company."* I hadn't thought about that before and it made the choice clearer that selling the company was the right decision for me.

A few considerations when soliciting life advice from others:

- Based on their own life experiences and biases, some people will be more comfortable taking risks, while others will be more conservative and safe than you are, so factor that in when evaluating their advice.
- Not all advice should be weighted equally. If you really look up to the person and they have given you solid advice in the past, their opinion may carry more weight than someone else's opinion.
- Too much of anything is generally bad, and that includes getting advice. It's easy to become overwhelmed and confused when there are "too many cooks in the kitchen," which can send you into a state of anxiety and frustration.

Remember, you are simply bouncing ideas off of your trusted advisors to help *you* think about *your* choices, so don't forget to also seek input from yourself. Take yourself on a mini-retreat and listen to your inner voice. This might mean a long walk in nature, a weekend in a hotel by yourself, or sitting at the laundromat (one of my favorite places to think!).

Make your own decision even if it's different from all the advice you sought out. It's your life, not theirs.

6. Evaluate the option of doing nothing. A mentor once told me, *"Don't make decisions until you have to. Then make them swiftly."* I have found this to be sage advice. We often sweat over impending decisions that don't need to be made. These decisions are still "in the percolator"—we likely don't yet have all the facts, and things can change before it's time to make the decision. One example of this is a teenager trying to decide what they want to be when they grow up. This life-changing decision can be delayed for several years. Sometimes not making a decision is the best decision.

When you try to make a decision too early, it leads to anticipatory anxiety because you don't have all the information you need to make a good decision...yet.

Dr. Ellen Ranger, a professor of psychology at Harvard, talks about instead of making the "right" decision, make the decision "right" for you. She tells a story about a student that stresses over whether to go to Harvard or Yale. The student chooses. Here is an excerpt from an interview where she explains why hypothetical regret won't get you anywhere.

"Rather than waste your time being stressed over making the right decision make the decision right. Randomly choose. Now, you can randomly choose if you want an Almond Joy or a Snickers, nobody's going to care. It's the exact same thing about getting married or not, taking the job or not. You can only live one life. If there were some magical way that I could live a life as somebody who's had three kids and somebody who hasn't had kids, maybe I can make a comparison. But you don't have that available to you. So I say to my students, 'Should you go to Harvard or should you go to Yale?' Let's say they made a decision to go to Harvard and let's say it's terrible. 'Oh, I wish I had gone to Yale.' There's no way of knowing that Yale wouldn't have been worse, better, or the same. That's why regret is so mindless because the choice you didn't take you're presuming would have been better."

It's a waste of energy to wonder if the other choice would have been better or worse because there is no way of knowing if that is true.

7. Don't be afraid to make a new decision. The good news about decisions is if you don't like one choice, you can make a new one. No one is going to stop you. You control the situation. If you don't like where you are, make a decision and change your course.

Many people wait for a magical surge of confidence to appear before making a decision. They think, *"I'll make this decision when I'm confident that I know what to do."* But that's not how confidence works.

Confidence often shows up after you make the decision and experience the outcome, not before.

When Decisions Go Bad

Once you start embracing your ability to make decisions, it will be impossible to avoid the occasional bad decision. The only way to avoid making bad decisions is to stop making decisions altogether (which in itself is actually a decision). Making decisions is hard, scary, and stressful, especially when navigating unknown territory, but realize there aren't really any "bad decisions." There are just decisions that didn't result in the current desired outcome.

> *What matters is not that you fail or make a mistake,*
> *but what you learn from it and how you do things*
> *differently as a result.*

Sometimes, the best outcomes come from what feel like the worst decisions. In the early days of my tech company, I was convinced that a two-way chat feature between pet owners and veterinary practices was a terrible idea. I pictured inboxes overflowing with endless questions and practices overwhelmed by the constant buzz of messages. I argued my case passionately to anyone who would listen. No way were we investing time or money into building such a flawed feature.

But then, the requests from our customers kept rolling in, and my team started pushing back. They brought up real examples of how this feature could actually make our clients' jobs easier and more efficient. It became clear that I had made the wrong call. I had to swallow my pride, pivot, and build out the very feature I had stubbornly resisted. And wouldn't you know it—the two-way chat feature became one of the biggest successes on our platform.

But let me tell you, bad decisions don't just happen in business—they happen in life, too. Take my first marriage, for example. I was three years into what had become an increasingly difficult relationship when it hit me: I had married the wrong guy. A divorce seemed like the end of the world, but I knew it had to be done. I felt depressed and defeated. I buried myself in work and focused on figuring out who I really was with a therapist.

A few years later, when I least expected it, I met the guy that was a perfect match for me. Looking back now, two things stand out from that time when I felt so lost and hopeless:

1. I was quietly growing into my own best friend.
2. I had to let go of something that wasn't right to make space for something better.

The wrong decisions often teach us the most important lessons, pushing us toward the growth we never knew we needed. Whether it's in business or in life, sometimes the best move you can make is to recognize when you're wrong, pivot, and open yourself up to the possibilities that come next. Here are a few strategies to recover from a bad decision:

Recognize that you have made a decision that resulted in an different outcome than expected. There are two ways you can approach a situation when the decision you made fails to deliver the outcome you were striving for in the first place:

- Dig in and push harder. You never want to quit too early. There are many decisions in life where the road to success is the more difficult one, so giving up too early may result in never achieving your true potential.
- Realize that you are on the wrong road and admit that your initial decision was a bad one.

How do you know when it's time to pivot? Try taking a step back and revisit why you made that decision in the first place. Do those reasons still hold up? Maybe something has shifted, and there's new information you didn't have before. Or perhaps you've grown since making that choice and now see things differently. When you take the time to reassess, you can catch when it's time to adjust course.

Reroute yourself. Just like your map on your smartphone, reroute yourself when you make a wrong turn. The earlier you figure out and admit to yourself that you are on the wrong road, the easier it will be for you to reset the course. Take the time to evaluate your next move and choose a new direction that better aligns with where you want to go.

Put your new plan into action. Once you recognize that you've made a bad decision and have a new plan, make a swift course correction. You don't want to waste any more of your time and energy going down the wrong road. If this requires difficult conversations, have them. If this requires hard work, do it. The good stuff—the really, really good stuff—requires taking action, tapping into your inner grit, and committing to do the hard things. The easy road leads to mediocrity, but the hard road often leads to huge success.

The Bottom Line

Being decisive isn't just about making choices—it's about owning your life and stepping into your potential. It's a skill that strengthens with practice. Every decision you make builds your confidence and sets the course for where you want your life to go. Remember, whether a decision turns out great or not, it brings valuable lessons and opportunities. In the end, the power to shape your path lies in the choices you make.

"You have to believe in yourself when no one else does."

— Serena Williams

KNOW YOUR NUMBERS

Success is more than just ambition or hard work—it's a numbers game. Every goal you're chasing likely has a financial equation attached to it, so knowing your numbers is essential. Yet, many women shy away from diving into their finances. We've been conditioned to avoid "boring" financial details, leaving the spreadsheets to someone else (usually a man). But let's get real: that mindset doesn't serve us anymore. It's time to shake off the dust, stop acting like a girl, and face the numbers in your life head-on.

I've been there. Fresh out of college and diving into my career, I didn't have a clue about investment funds, mortgages, or all those things you're "supposed to know." It felt overwhelming, boring, and like something I could put off for later. But trust me, the time to face it is now. The sooner you take control of your finances, the more freedom you'll gain—and having the freedom to live life on your terms is one of the most empowering things you can do for yourself.

Historically, money management was always "the man's job" as head of the household, and it wasn't until the 1980s that women were even allowed to have their own credit cards without a male cosigner. No wonder so many women are hesitant to take charge of their finances—we weren't even trusted with it until a few decades ago. But we've come a long way since then. It is your responsibility to know your earning potential, how investments work, and what to do with your money. If you're lucky enough to afford a financial advisor, great. But even then, stay involved. And if hiring help isn't an option, guess what? You can absolutely handle this yourself. It's not as hard as it seems, but like all good things, it takes a little time and effort.

It's your life. You can't expect anyone else to care more about it than you.

The Top 3 Numbers Every Woman Needs To Know

1. Your Personal Finances

In my twenties and thirties, thinking about getting old felt like a distant reality. But here's the truth: If you're lucky, you will get older, and you don't want to run out of money before the race is over. Understanding your personal financial situation is the first step toward securing the kind of freedom, comfort, and lifestyle you dream about.

Start by thinking about the end game. I'll never forget when my male business partner asked, *"What's your number?"* I tilted my head, totally puzzled. He meant how much money I needed to live my dream life—the lifestyle I envisioned but had never fully mapped out. This is something I had never thought about.

> **Here's an exercise he gave me:** *Picture your dream life. What kind of lifestyle do you want? Do you want to clear debts, fund a family member's education, or even retire early in some picturesque setting? What do you want your golden years to look like? Break it all down and add up the costs. That's your number—your financial target.*

Now, figure out what it will take to reach it and decide if you're willing to put in the work. This will help you know when to stay and fight or when it's time to move on if the job, or situation, isn't right for you.

Knowing your financial goal and actually reaching it are two different things. Think of your life as a business, and you're the CEO. The main goal? Achieving financial freedom as soon as possible, because it's one of the most empowering things a woman can do for herself. It gives you independence and puts you in full control of your life. You won't have to depend on anyone to support you or make decisions for you —you'll be in the driver's seat. Here are some other key benefits you will experience by gaining financial independence:

Ability to leave toxic situations: Whether it's a toxic workplace or a bad relationship, having financial security allows you to walk away from negative environments. You won't feel trapped because you have the ability to support yourself.

Less stress and anxiety: Financial freedom brings peace of mind. You're less likely to worry about unexpected expenses, bills, or the future when you have savings, investments, and a financial plan in place. This reduces stress and allows you to focus on other areas of your life.

Increased confidence: Knowing you're financially secure builds confidence, and it's one of the best ways to combat imposter syndrome. Being able to pay for your own life gives you the freedom to care less about what others think. You can focus on your own goals and desires without worrying about fitting into someone else's expectations.

Freedom to invest in yourself: Financial stability allows you to invest in your personal growth, whether through education, travel, or self-care. You can afford to take courses, explore new hobbies, or prioritize your health—all of which make your life better.

Ability to help others: When you achieve financial freedom, you are now in a spot to give back to family, friends, and causes that matter to you. Whether it's contributing to a charity you're passionate about, supporting a friend in need, or volunteering your time for a cause you believe in, you can make a real difference. Plus, here's the secret: Helping others often lifts your own spirits the most. It's a win-win.

Ultimately, achieving financial freedom takes focus and hard work—unless, of course, you're lucky enough to inherit a fortune. For most people though, gaining financial freedom means being disciplined and making smart financial choices. Here are some key steps to get you on the right path:

Start budgeting early. First things first, create a simple budget to see where your money's going. Break it down so you can easily manage what you earn and spend. Try the 50/30/20 rule: 50% for needs (rent, car payment), 30% for fun (shopping, going to restaurants), and 20% for savings and debt payments. This keeps you balanced without sacrificing too much.

Build your safety net. Aim to save three to six months of living expenses in an emergency fund. Think of it as your financial cushion for life's unexpected twists— whether it's a surprise bill or a job switch.

Live below your means. As your income grows, resist the urge to splurge. It's tempting to upgrade everything, but keeping your expenses in check means you'll have more to save and invest. Your future self will thank you.

Get rid of high-interest debt. If you've got credit card or loan debt with high interest rates, focus on paying it off ASAP. The longer it sits, the more it grows—and not in a good way. Try the snowball method (tackle the smallest debts first) or the avalanche method (go after the highest interest debts).

Start investing—like, yesterday. One of the best things you can do is start investing early. Even small amounts add up over time thanks to compound interest. If you've got access to a 401(k) or IRA, jump on it.

Set it and forget it. Automate your savings and bill payments so you don't have to think about it. This way, you're consistently saving and won't be hit with any late fees. Have a percentage of your paycheck go directly into your savings or investment accounts. This makes it easier to stick to your goals.

Cover yourself with insurance. Make sure you're covered for life's curveballs. Health insurance is a must, but also look into renters or homeowners insurance, and auto insurance. You want to be protected from big surprise expenses that could knock you off track.

Don't play the comparison game. Social media can make it seem like everyone else is living the dream, but remember, your journey is yours. Stick to your own financial plan and don't fall into the trap of trying to keep up with others.

Boost your credit score. A good credit score is your ticket to better financial opportunities. Pay your bills on time, keep your credit card balances low, and check your score regularly to ensure everything's in good shape.

When you make your own money, you get to call the shots in your life and the opinions of others become less significant.

For someone in their 40s or beyond looking for financial independence, it's good to remember that it's never too late to take charge of your financial future. Just because you're starting later doesn't mean you've missed your chance, as it can be a great opportunity to reassess your goals, learn from past experiences, and create the life you want.

However, if you're in your 20s or 30s and reading this, take a moment to appreciate the amazing opportunity in front of you. Don't put it off. Starting your financial journey now means you can set yourself up for success to chase your dreams and live life on your terms. And, if you're smart about it, you can most likely achieve millionaire status by the time you hit your 60s.

	Earn	Spend	Build Wealth
Early Career 20s-30s	• Start full-time employment. • Get settled into a career. • Explore additional income sources, like side gigs or freelancing, if you can't make ends meet.	• Start paying off student loans and other debts. • Cover basic living expenses, like rent, utilities, and food. • Establish a 3-6 month emergency fund.	• Start investing in retirement accounts, like a 401(k) or IRA. • Set financial goals and budgets. • Start to invest in the stock market. • Purchase insurance.
Mid Career 30s-40s	• Advance in your career and increase earnings. • Look for opportunities for bonuses and stock options with your company.	• Buy a home. • Manage expenses, like education and childcare. • Increase insurance coverage. Consider life and disability policies.	• Maximize retirement contributions. • Diversify your investments, considering real estate, stocks, and bonds. • Continue education and career development.
Peak Earning 40s-50s	• Reach your highest salary levels. • Explore passive income streams, like rental properties and dividends.	• Pay off significant debts, like mortgages. • Aggressively pay down all debts. • Increase discretionary spending on travel or other hobbies.	• Invest in tax-advantaged accounts. • Plan for the future by establishing wills and trusts.
Pre-Retirement 50s-60s	• Continue peak earning or transition to part-time work. • Manage investments and passive income.	• Prepare for reduced income in retirement. • Expect higher healthcare costs. • Potentially help support aging parents or adult children.	• Finalize retirement plans. • Adjust investment portfolio for lower risk. • Conduct detailed estate planning and tax strategies.
Retirement 60s and beyond	• Draw income from retirement accounts • Begin collecting Social Security benefits. • Consider possible part-time work or consulting.	• Live on a fixed income. • Manage healthcare and long-term care costs. • Enjoy a leisurely lifestyle.	• Ensure sustainable withdrawal rates from retirement accounts. • Adjust investments to ensure the longevity of funds. • Plan for your legacy and end-of-life.

2. Your Company's Finances

Whether you're starting out as an entry-level employee or working your way up the ladder, understanding your company's finances is essential to getting noticed and advancing your career. Even if you're not a CEO or manager, mastering the numbers behind your department's budget, revenue goals, and expenses can set you apart and highlight you as a leader-in-the-making.

When you start paying attention to the financial health of the company, you're not just doing your job—you're showing that you think like an owner. This kind of mindset doesn't go unnoticed by those above you. When leaders see that you understand how the business runs and are invested in its success, they're more likely to view you as someone who's ready for more responsibility.

So, how do you start getting a grip on your company's numbers, especially when you don't have access to the full financial picture? Begin by learning as much as possible about the finances directly impacting your role and department. How does your team contribute to the company's revenue? What are the costs associated with running your department? Understanding these basics can help you identify areas for improvement, like cutting unnecessary expenses or finding ways to boost productivity. When you bring solutions based on numbers, people notice.

Let's be real—most entry to mid-level employees don't walk into meetings armed with budget sheets and financial reports. But imagine if you did. Before your next team meeting, take the initiative to gather and review the key financials related to your role or department. Even if you're not directly responsible for the budget, knowing these numbers and being prepared to discuss them gives you a huge advantage. It signals to others that you're thinking ahead and that you have the potential to lead.

Here's a strategy: Even if you're not yet in a position to control a budget, ask questions. Go to your manager and express interest in how the department is performing financially. Say something like, *"I want to understand more about how our team contributes to the company's bottom line—can you walk me through some of the key numbers?"* This will not only give you valuable insight but also show your manager that you're serious about growth.

Also, learn the lingo. Financial conversations can feel like a foreign language if you're not used to them. Terms like "EBITDA," "cash flow," or "ROI" may seem intimidating at first, but they're critical to making smart decisions. Don't wait until you're in a leadership position to start learning. Take the initiative now to educate yourself on these concepts, whether through online courses, reading, or asking for help from someone who knows their stuff. The more you understand the language of business, the easier it will be to navigate high-level conversations and contribute meaningfully.

Once you are on the rise from being a mid-level employee to an upper-level employee, there are some key metrics to master. These are often referred to as key performance indicators (KPIs). These numbers are more than just figures on a spreadsheet; they're a roadmap to where the business is heading. Some of the primary KPIs include:

- **Revenue Growth Rate:** Are sales increasing at a healthy pace year over year?
- **Profit Margins:** Understand both gross and net profit margins. What's being left after costs?
- **Operating Cash Flow:** How much cash is the business actually generating from its operations?

- **Customer Acquisition Cost (CAC):** What does it cost to gain a new customer?
- **Lifetime Value (LTV):** How much revenue does each customer generate throughout their relationship with the company?

You will also need to be familiar with the following common business processes:

Annual budgeting. Most companies set annual budgets, but truly successful leaders monitor and adjust throughout the year. As part of this, learn to differentiate between fixed and variable costs. Fixed costs (like rent and salaries) remain the same, while variable costs (like marketing expenses and utilities) fluctuate depending on sales volume. Understanding this helps in identifying areas to cut back on during lean times or where to allocate extra resources when revenue is strong.

Forecasting and financial planning. Forecasting is like your business's crystal ball. It predicts future revenues, expenses, and profits based on current data and trends. Even if you don't work directly with the company's finances, you can position yourself as an invaluable asset by learning how to project future outcomes in your department or team. Being proactive rather than reactive to change is what separates strong leaders from everyone else.

Expense management. Expenses can quietly bleed a company dry if not managed correctly. Developing a mindset of financial discipline within your team or department goes a long way. This could mean being more strategic about sourcing vendors, monitoring spending patterns for inefficiencies, or finding creative ways to boost productivity without significant cost increases.

Building a culture of financial accountability. Whether you're leading a small team or an entire company, fostering a culture where everyone is aware of how their actions impact the bottom line is crucial. When employees know that their decisions affect profitability, they're more likely to make choices aligned with business goals. For example, if you're in a leadership role, share financial updates during team meetings. Transparency leads to buy-in, and buy-in leads to a sense of ownership, where everyone feels responsible for the company's success.

Data-driven decision making. Numbers tell a story—

they highlight strengths, expose weaknesses, and point the way forward. Ensure that you're not making gut decisions based solely on instincts or intuition. Use data as a foundation for your strategy. A well-informed decision backed by numbers is always more persuasive and effective.

Lastly, don't underestimate the power of preparation. When the opportunity arises for you to be in the room where financial discussions happen, make sure you're ready. Review your notes, anticipate questions, and think about how you can add value to the conversation. This is how you transition from being just another employee to someone who stands out as leadership material.

3. Your Wage

One of your biggest assets is your ability to earn money. But when it comes to equal pay, unfortunately, the gender gap is still alive and well. According to the Federal Register, as of 2024, women make 84 cents to every dollar a man earns. One reason for this could be that many women struggle with asking for a raise. Most women treat a raise like a magical gift being bestowed upon them by their employer. One of the biggest reasons you may not be getting a raise is because your employer isn't thinking about you. They are dealing with bigger issues for the business and you aren't top of mind for them. It's up to you to take charge and advocate for yourself.

Here is a step-by-step action plan to get a raise:

1. Know what you're worth, and know the market.
Simply "wanting a raise" is too vague—try to be clear on exactly how much you want to earn. The main reason many people don't get what they want is that they're not specific enough in their request.

You've probably heard that saying in real estate: *"A house is worth what someone is willing to pay for it."* The same applies to you. Many women hesitate to ask for a raise because they feel they aren't skilled enough or still need to improve. They keep waiting to be better or more qualified before making the ask, but that mindset often holds them back.

Instead, ask yourself, *"What would this company do if I wasn't here tomorrow? Would they be in a jam without me?"* This is your value to the business—not how much schooling you had, how many years you have been with the company, or your age.

It is also important to do market research on the average salary for your job. Reach out to others in your field to discuss salary and benefits. But don't just ask other women, ask the men since they typically make more than women for the same job. If you are concerned that asking your coworkers what they earn will be awkward and viewed negatively by leadership, go outside your company and check with others in similar roles or consult online tools, like Glass Door, that publish average salaries by role.

Think of a job as a stepping stone, with each stone getting you one step closer to what you want to earn. When you know your number, you will know when you've made it to the top. Each time you hit the compensation ceiling in a role, ask yourself if this is good enough. If it's not, look around. Look up, down, to the left, and to the right. Sometimes the next step requires a detour. One of the worst things you can do is stay in a job that will never be able to pay you what you want. It will most likely lead to frustration, stress, and negativity.

This happened to me in my first job as a veterinarian. I spent six years working at an emergency practice in Portland, Oregon, and I reached a dead end. I wanted to earn more money and I wanted a better lifestyle. My detour took me to a new job in Colorado with a 20% pay cut, but it unlocked a clear path up, and within two years I was able to make more money and have more opportunities than I had with the first job. Sometimes climbing up means taking a few steps backward first.

2. Set the stage. If you want to maximize your earning potential, you've got to set the stage well in advance. The last thing you want is to be blindsided by negative feedback when you think you're doing a great job. I'll never forget a time when I felt confident in my performance, only to discover my boss saw things very differently. I was going through my divorce at the time and didn't realize the stress was affecting my work. It was a harsh wake-up call—one I wish I'd known about before walking in to ask for a raise.

Starting about three to six months in advance, begin checking in with your supervisor every month to ask, *"Is there anything you would like to see me do differently or better? I'm always eager to improve."* If they have feedback, discuss, and act on it. Then, follow up with your supervisor to get their input on your progress. Demonstrate that you are teachable and coachable.

This will show your boss that you are a go-getter and set the expectation that you are not someone who settles.

Keep track of your wins, successes, and triumphs. Did you start a journal club for you and your colleagues? Write it down! Did you take an online course? Track it! Did you come up with a way to save the business some money or a way to increase revenue? Record that! You can mention these triumphs when you meet with your boss to request a raise.

Pro tip: As a boss, I can count on one hand the people who took the time to express concern or recognize the efforts I was putting forth as a leader. Keep your leaders in mind regularly. Send them a card on "Boss's Day," drop the occasional thank-you card in the mail, or just tell them you appreciate their efforts. Let them know that you see them and all they are doing. That appreciation will go a long way, especially when it comes to deciding who is getting a raise that year.

3. Time it right. Hopefully, you work for a company that regularly reviews performance and salary, but if you don't, request a meeting with your boss several weeks in advance. Do not spring this on your boss.

They need time to mentally prepare for the conversation. Instead, send an email to your boss that says something like this:

"Please let me know a good time for you and me to meet in the next few weeks. I would like to discuss my salary and the next steps for getting a raise. I've included my history of raises and a list of accomplishments for your convenience. Thanks so much, <your name>"

Here's another important tip: Pay attention to your boss's routines and moods. When are they typically in the best spirits? Fridays, for instance, might not be ideal since end-of-week fatigue can affect their mood. The same goes for late in the day when energy levels dip. Aim to schedule your meeting when they're rested, well-fed, and in a positive mindset. And if things go sideways before your scheduled time—a crisis pops up, for example—don't be afraid to reschedule. Stack the odds in your favor!

4. Say the words. In this situation, it's best to communicate directly and effectively. Words matter. You want to convey confidence in your request for a raise without sounding arrogant. The most effective employees I have ever managed said something like this:

"Thank you for meeting with me. I'm excited to talk with you about my official request for a raise."

Then, proceed with a short recap of three accomplishments in the last six months to further validate your request for a raise.

"I really appreciate you meeting with me regularly these last six months so I could do my part to keep the company on course. Recently, I am most proud of the 42 night shifts I worked on call, the $500K in revenue I brought in, and the extra time I spent mentoring our new vet."

Then, set the expectation by saying:

"I would like to have a compensation conversation. Is now a good time to talk about that? Do you prefer to discuss this in person, or is email better?"

By saying it this way, you are recognizing that your boss may not be ready at that moment to have the conversation. You are showing that you are flexible and thoughtful of their situation but are in pursuit of having the conversation.

Your boss may be ready to have the conversation, so be prepared. When the time is right, either now or later, when the moment presents itself, put your shoulders back, straighten your crown, and say these words:

"I would like to officially request a raise of X dollars."

Next, take a drink of your water and shut up. The next person to speak should be your boss. You will be nervous and want to fill the quiet space with babble, but don't. This strategy is called the "power of the pause," and while it might be the most uncomfortable thing you've ever done, it will also emphasize your point, allow your boss to process what you said, and reflect confidence and composure.

5. Play the long game. After you ask for a raise, you will experience one of the following outcomes:

- **Your boss agrees and gives you the raise.** Woo-hoo! Before you dash off to Amazon, take a few minutes to write your boss a thank-you note. Acknowledge how much you appreciate working for a company that values you. In addition to being basic good manners, this will stand out to your boss and make them inclined to say yes next year when you ask for another raise.

- **Your boss declines** and, through various possible explanations, lets you know you are not going to get a raise. Instead of going off the rails or spiraling down a rabbit hole, ask your boss this question: *"What would need to happen for me to get the raise?"* This will help you understand how close (or far) you are from getting the raise and give you a goal mark. Good communication is key here. Don't just accept no for an answer. Find out what it's going to take to move up in salary, and then start climbing. Make sure what needs to happen translates into tangible goals to accomplish. Write them down during the meeting. Then, follow up with an email to confirm that "x, y, z" needs to happen before you get a raise equal to X dollars and ask them to respond. Then, you have it in writing and, when you complete that list, you can ask for another meeting, bring the list, and explain or demonstrate how you have accomplished each of the goals.

- **Your boss negotiates with you for a lower raise.** This one is tricky. It's important to understand why you won't be getting the raise you asked for, so be sure to ask: *"What needs to happen for me to get the full raise?"* Maybe you need to advance your skills, take on more responsibilities, or learn something new that could directly impact revenue. Ask yourself, *"What can I bring to the table that would improve my value to the company?"* In addition, try to negotiate a gradual raise. For example, if your boss says that the company can only afford to give you half of what you asked for, then ask for the rest of the raise to roll out in six months. You could say it like this: *"OK, I understand. I also want to balance the company's needs with my own. Do you think we could do half of the raise now and the other half in six months?"* Even if they say no, it's worth a try.

The key to getting a raise is pushing through the discomfort, advocating for yourself, and taking the Nike approach: Just do it! What's the worst that could happen? They say no. You'll survive. Even if you don't get the answer you want, you'll walk away stronger and more confident because you faced that uncomfortable conversation with professionalism and poise. Each time you do, you're one step closer to getting what you deserve.

The Bottom Line

Mastering your finances isn't just about having more zeros in your bank account—it's about unlocking the freedom to live life on your terms. When you take control of your money, you take control of your future. Financial independence is more than just a dream; it's a necessity for anyone serious about success. By understanding your numbers, owning your worth, and positioning yourself for growth, you can break free from the outdated mindset that has held so many women back. Remember, you're not just crunching numbers—you're shaping the life you want.

"The best way to make a difference in the world is to start making a difference in your own life."

— Julia Louis-Dreyfus

ASK FOR WHAT YOU WANT

Getting what you want in life comes down to two simple but powerful steps: first, getting clear on what you really want, and second, finding the courage to ask for it. While identifying what you want can be a challenge for almost everyone, regardless of gender, the act of asking for it is where many women hit a wall. It's not that women don't know what they want—instead, they have been conditioned from a young age to hold back. As girls, many of us were taught to be agreeable, to prioritize the needs of others, and to avoid being perceived as too demanding or assertive. This conditioning can cross over into adulthood, making the simple act of asking for what we want feel daunting or even selfish.

But the truth is, asking for what you want is not just about getting what you desire—it's about claiming your space, owning your voice, and stepping into the life you deserve. This chapter will explore both of these steps: identifying your desires and, just as importantly, learning to ask for them without hesitation. It's time to unlearn the habits that hold us back and embrace the power that comes with asking for what you want.

Identify What You Want

What do you want? It's a simple question with layers of complexity that can be easy to dodge. Here are a few reasons why you might be avoiding answering it:

- You have self-doubt.
- You feel uncertain or overwhelmed by choices.
- You fear choosing the wrong path.
- You're waiting for the "right time" (graduating, getting that promotion, starting a family).
- You're waiting for a sign from the universe.

When you avoid answering the question, *What do I want in life?* you're like a boat adrift in a stormy sea, tossed wherever the waves decide to take you.

Without a clear destination, you're never going to reach where you want to go.

If you are struggling to figure out what you want in life, here are three exercises that might help you get unstuck:

1. The Perfect Day Exercise[1]

Imagine your perfect day from start to finish. Where do you wake up? Who is with you? What do you do? How do you feel? Write down every detail from the morning to the night, focusing on the environment, activities, and people around you. This visualization can highlight what truly brings you joy and fulfillment.

2. Strengths and Passions Inventory[2]

Make two lists: one of your strengths (things you're naturally good at) and one of your passions (things you love doing). Where do they overlap? The intersection of your strengths and passions can be a good indicator of the kind of life and work that would fulfill you.

3. The Life Wheel[3]

Draw a circle divided into eight sections representing key

life areas (e.g., career, family, health, personal growth, relationships, finances, fun, and contribution). Rate your current satisfaction in each area from one to ten. Then, reflect on the areas that need the most attention and what changes would increase your overall life satisfaction.

The only wrong answer to the "What do I want?" question is avoiding it altogether. Stop waiting for perfect clarity or that ideal moment to decide. Instead, answer based on what you know about yourself in this moment. Identify your current goal and let it become your North Star, guiding every decision you make. And here's a liberating truth: you can change your course anytime.

Your destiny is written in pencil, not ink.

Once you know your destination, you can use it to guide both big and small decisions. When faced with any choice, ask yourself, "Is this bringing me closer to or further from my North Star?" This mindset turns your daily decisions into steps toward the life of your dreams.

Surround Yourself With The Right People

To get what you want, you'll need to have the right people in your corner. It's critical to surround yourself with people who are going in the same general direction you are going, or maybe they have already arrived where you hope to be someday. The crowd you associate with helps develop and strengthen your thoughts and energy around ambition, skill, confidence, and drive. If you want to learn how to ski black diamonds, you don't get there by hitting the slopes with people who can only do the bunny slopes—you ski with people who excel at black diamonds.

Take a look at your current circle. Who are the black diamonds? If you find yourself outpacing your peers, it might be time to broaden your network. Surrounding yourself with others who elevate and challenge you helps you grow stronger and more confident.

Another great thing about being around powerhouse people is that you'll start to see they're not all that different from you. The people you admire and think have more skills or talents? They're regular people, just like you.

You are just as deserving of success as anyone else.

If you're like most people, you're going to have moments of self-doubt and anxiety, and that nagging fear of failure. That's just imposter syndrome creeping in, and honestly, unless you're a complete sociopath, everyone goes through it. It's totally normal, especially when you're trying something new. But here's the thing: After you do it once—then again and again—that feeling starts to fade. That's how your confidence grows, by putting in the reps and getting that experience under your belt. Building confidence in something requires a mix of practice, the right mindset, and patience—and it often means facing what scares you head-on.

Confidence shows up after you have faced what scares you, not before.

Trust Your Inner Voice

We all have that quiet inner voice—a whisper of truth and guidance. Some call it intuition or a spiritual guide, but regardless of what you name it, it's there to support you. This voice doesn't shout and it is easily drowned out by the noise of your life. It requires you to carefully listen.

To really connect with your inner voice, you need to quiet your mind and clear out distractions. Often, this voice is easy to dismiss because it may tell us things we don't want to hear.

When you take the time to listen to your inner voice, you are embracing your best friend. And that best friend is you.

Your inner voice is not there to criticize or tear you down. It's there to guide you, give you strength, and remind you of your worth. Don't allow negative thoughts to hijack it. If your inner voice has been suppressed by years of negativity, it might take some effort to rediscover it through meditation, therapy, or other practices. Remember, that voice only wants the best for you and never leads you toward failure.

Do not use your inner voice to be mean to yourself. It wasn't made for that. Your little voice loves you. It's there to help you pick up the pieces when your life is falling apart. It's there to give you strength when you have none. It's there to hold your hand when you feel lonely. Do not abuse your little voice by manipulating it to talk negatively to yourself. Life is negative enough—there is no need to add more.

Here are some examples of what your little voice should be saying to you:

- *"I am capable of achieving my goals."*
- *"I am worthy of love and respect."*
- *"I am grateful for the blessings in my life."*

- *"I believe in my ability to overcome challenges."*
- *"I am confident in myself and my abilities."*
- *"I am deserving of happiness and fulfillment."*
- *"I am enough just as I am."*

Your inner voice may have been hijacked by your brain if you're hearing:

- *"I'm not good enough."*
- *"I'll never succeed."*
- *"I'm worthless."*
- *"Nobody cares about me."*
- *"I'm always messing things up."*
- *"I'll never be happy."*
- *"I'm not smart/talented/creative enough."*

If you're hearing these phrases, first you must realize that this is not your little voice, and you need to take steps to find it, like meditation, therapy, or medication. You will probably need help locating your inner voice because it can go dormant and hide inside the corners of your mind, especially if it has been getting beaten up for years. Your little voice only wants you to succeed—it never wants you to fail.

Your inner voice will guide you and help you determine exactly what you want and where you want to go in life.

Ask For What You Want

Once you've identified what you want, the next step is learning to ask for it. When women are demure, shy, or constantly prioritize the needs of others, they often end up sacrificing their own desires and ambitions. This can lead to resentment, frustration, and a sense of regret.

Asking for what you want is not only about getting what you need or desire—it also signals to yourself and others that your voice matters, your goals are valid, and your contributions are valuable. It sets a precedent that you are in control of your own life and that you are willing to advocate for yourself, just as you would for others.

Being assertive and clear about your wants doesn't mean you lack kindness or consideration for others. Instead, it means you're giving yourself permission to be an equal player in your own life. By asking for what you want, you also pave the way for other women to do the same, breaking the cycle of self-sacrifice that has held many back for so long. When women step up and voice their needs, they create opportunities for growth, both personally and professionally, and help shift societal norms towards greater equality and respect for all voices.

Here are some tips to start asking for what you want in the workplace, and in life:

Do your homework. Before you walk into a situation when you are going to ask for what you want, make sure you're ready. Gather all the info and relevant data you'll need. Pretend you are the other person and think of three questions they might ask. Then, practice your answers, just in case. The better prepared you are, the more confident you'll feel.

Choose empowering language. Drop the wishy-washy words. Be clear and direct when asking for what you want. Use phrases like:

- *"I want…"*
- *"I am requesting…"*
- *"I need…"*

Avoid vague phrases that undermine your message:

- *"I'm not sure, but…."*
- *"If it's not a problem…"*

Choose the right time. The best time to ask for something is when you are in a good headspace and aren't fire-engine red mad over it. When you're angry, you are at risk of going off the rails and not thinking clearly. If you have to discuss and debate the issue to get what you want, anger will limit your ability to find the right words and think of examples to build your case and win the discussion.

Also, choose the time of day that you have the most mental clarity. By knowing yourself, you will know if you do your best thinking in the morning or afternoon, after the gym, or after a snack and a giant quad shot of coffee. Whenever it is, set yourself up for success by having the conversation when you are in your prime state.

Read the room. Not everyone sees things the way you do. Something that may be crystal clear to you will be blurry to someone else. Each person has their own perspective based on their thoughts and beliefs. Understand the other person is likely coming to the table with an entirely different point of view. Your job is to meet people where they are, seek to understand their perspectives, and then choose the right approach to move your agenda forward.

Bring the confidence. It helps you present your case clearly and shows that you truly believe in what you are asking for. Make sure to bring the best version of yourself to the table. You know yourself better than anyone, so do what it takes to get in the right mindset before the conversation. For me, that means getting to bed early the night before, wearing a power color like red, and scheduling meetings first thing in the morning—waiting all day to have a tough talk gives me a stomachache.

Show respect. Keeping the conversation professional and respectful helps you make your point clearly, builds trust, and highlights your ability to handle business with strength and grace. This boosts the likelihood that your request will be taken seriously and demonstrates you have the skills and the manners to back them up. Personally, I like to put my hair up and imagine I'm wearing a crown. It's my way of channeling a queen's poise and grace, helping me stay composed and respectful, even in tough conversations.

Represent yourself. Growing up, many girls are taught to be humble and not brag about their accomplishments. While you definitely want to avoid coming off as arrogant, it's crucial to stand up for yourself and celebrate what you bring to the table. If talking about your achievements feels awkward, pretend you're speaking on behalf of your best friend. When you step outside your own insecurities and let go of the pressure to be modest, it's much easier to confidently showcase your skills and successes.

Don't let people gaslight you. To let someone gaslight you means you're allowing them to manipulate you into doubting your own perceptions, memories, or reality. For example, if someone constantly denies saying things you clearly remember them saying, or insists that something happened in a way it didn't, and you start to second-guess your own experiences, you're being gaslit. It's important to recognize gaslighting behavior and set boundaries to protect yourself in these situations.

When dealing with gaslighters, I've found that short, neutral responses work best. Try phrases like:

- *"Interesting"*
- *"I'm going to need to think about this."*
- *"I see it another way."*

Arguing with a gaslighter usually doesn't get you anywhere. It's better to keep your replies short and then approach the situation from a different angle at another time.

Showcase Your Strengths

Women often struggle with showcasing their strengths, and it's not surprising given the cultural and social hurdles they face. Many of us were taught to be modest and avoid boasting about our achievements, which can make it tough to speak up about our successes. There's also the worry of being seen as conceited or pushy, which can hold us back from claiming our space. Add to that the nagging self-doubt of imposter syndrome, and it is easy to see why promoting ourselves can feel so challenging.

But here's the thing: Overcoming these hurdles is essential for moving forward in our careers and lives. When you confidently highlight your strengths, you're not just patting yourself on the back—you're making sure that your contributions are recognized and valued. This can lead to new opportunities, promotions, and a boost in confidence. Plus, it helps to break down the barriers that keep women from advancing by changing the narrative around self-promotion and assertiveness.

When you showcase your achievements, it can inspire others to do the same. When you stand up and speak about your successes, without boasting or bragging, you set a positive example for those around you. This not only helps you grow but also fosters a work environment where everyone's talents are celebrated and valued. So, the next time you're tempted to downplay your achievements, remember that embracing and sharing them can pave the way for greater opportunities and help create a more inclusive workplace.

Here are a few strategic and tactful ways to weave your strengths, contributions, and accomplishments into conversations:

Frame it as a response to a question. If someone asks about your work or recent projects, use the opportunity to mention your accomplishments naturally as part of the conversation.

Share credit. When discussing accomplishments, acknowledge the contributions of your team or colleagues. This demonstrates humility and reflects positively on your ability to work collaboratively.

Focus on outcomes. Instead of simply listing your achievements, emphasize the positive outcomes or impacts of your work. Highlighting how your accomplishments benefited the team, project, or organization can make your contributions more meaningful.

Be specific and concise. Instead of providing a laundry list of accomplishments, choose a few key examples that are most relevant to the conversation and provide specific details about what you achieved and how.

Be humble. While it's important to showcase your accomplishments, it's equally important to remain humble and avoid appearing arrogant. Express gratitude for the opportunities you've had and the support you've received along the way.

Connect it to the topic at hand. Look for natural opportunities to mention your accomplishments within the context of the conversation. For example, if discussing a related topic or problem, you could mention how you successfully addressed a similar challenge in the past.

Seek feedback or advice. If appropriate, mention your accomplishments as a way to seek feedback or advice from others. For example, you could say, *"I recently completed a project where we achieved [specific outcome]. I'd love to hear your thoughts on how we can build on that success."*

Handle Rejection

Sometimes, even with the best approach, you won't get what you want. And that's OK. If you take enough shots, you are going to miss a few. Rejection is just redirection. Move forward by going back to the drawing board to plan your next move. This is a stepping stone, not an end, to your success.

*When you get turned down, it doesn't mean you failed,
it just means the timing isn't right.*

When you walk into a difficult conversation and don't get the result you were hoping for, it's crucial to handle the situation with a blend of grace and strategy. Here are some tips to help you do just that:

Stay composed. It's totally normal to feel let down when your request doesn't go as planned, but how you handle it can make all the difference. Staying calm and professional helps keep things on track and shows that you've got maturity and composure—traits that definitely boost your professional image. If you feel tears starting to well up, take a deep breath, grab a sip of water, and pull yourself together. Save the tears for later, maybe in the privacy of your car or the bathroom. Try to stay composed during the conversation—it's all part of showing that you can handle tough moments with grace.

Seek feedback. Once the decision has been made, it's time to dig into the details. Asking for feedback is about understanding the why behind the outcome. Find out what influenced the decision and why your request didn't hit the mark. This insight will help you pinpoint where you might need to adjust your approach or where you can improve.

Clarify next steps. Now that you have some feedback, figure out what concrete steps you can take to boost your chances next time. Ask for clear, actionable advice on how to move forward. If you learned that you need to acquire more skills in a certain area, make a game plan and get started. If you learned you need to stop doing something, take the steps necessary to do that.

Express appreciation. Regardless of the outcome, be sure to thank the person for their time and consideration. A genuine "thank you" reinforces your professionalism and shows respect for their role. It's a simple gesture that helps keep the door open for positive future interactions. Whether it's a quick thank-you message or a verbal expression of gratitude, it'll leave a lasting positive impression.

Do a postmortem. Take a moment to really reflect on what happened and dig into the feedback you received. Use it as a guide for improvement. Think about how you approached the situation, how well you prepared, and if there were any chances you missed. Maybe you wish you'd said something differently. Treat this as a valuable learning opportunity—what will you do differently to nail it next time?

Plan your next move. Now is the time to get strategic. Map out a timeline with clear goals and milestones to help you reach your next big step. Figure out exactly what you need to do, and break it down into manageable chunks—think monthly, weekly, and daily goals. It's the small, steady steps that will carry you forward and get you closer to where you want to be.

Ditch The People Pleasing

When you start speaking up for yourself, don't be surprised if it makes some people uncomfortable. They might call you "difficult," "bossy," or "arrogant," but don't let their labels get to you. Remember, their reactions are their problem, not yours. Society often teaches girls to seek approval and be liked by everyone, while it seems like guys have a different mindset—they don't worry so much about whether others like them.

The problem with the desire to be liked is that it can lead you to putting yourself second, which can be a real roadblock to reaching your goals. It's great to be kind and respectful, but the reality is, not everyone will be a fan of yours. Just like you have people you don't click with, some people won't click with you. Focus on living with kindness, respect, and integrity. If someone doesn't like you, that's OK—just move on and keep being yourself. Choose authenticity over approval.

Everyone won't like you. You're not pizza.

This doesn't mean there's anything wrong with you. It doesn't mean you're not good enough, pretty enough, or smart enough. Sometimes, personalities don't mesh. With over seven billion people in the world, you're bound to find plenty of people who "get" you and appreciate you just as you are. Don't let this small mismatch play out in your head and mess with your confidence.

Know When To Walk Away

Sometimes, no matter how hard you try, it feels like you're a round peg trying to fit into a square hole. Maybe the company culture isn't right or you've been consistently passed over for promotions. It could be that you're stuck in a toxic environment where your efforts to make a change are met with resistance.

If you're feeling undervalued and unappreciated, it's a sign that it might be time to move on.

Leaving a familiar job or situation, even one that's not ideal, can be an overwhelming thought. The fear of the unknown can make it hard to take the leap. However, staying in an environment where you're not recognized or supported can seriously impact your physical and mental health. There are many physical ailments that can be signs of a toxic environment. Here are a few:

- Constantly feeling drained and exhausted
- Frequent headaches or migraines
- Digestive issues like stomachaches and diarrhea
- Trouble sleeping
- Changes in your weight

And then there are the mental health signs:

- Constant anxiety and stress
- Loss of interest in activities you used to enjoy
- Irritability and mood swings
- Preferring isolation to socializing

- Social media addiction

Recognize that your well-being is worth more than the comfort of the status quo. If you're constantly dreading work or feeling trapped, it's time to start exploring new opportunities where you can truly thrive and feel valued. At the very least, begin looking around to see what options might be out there for you.

The Bottom Line

Asking for what you want isn't just about getting things; it's about showing yourself how much you matter. When you know what you want and ask for it confidently, you're taking control of your life. The path to your dreams won't always be smooth—there'll be bumps and rejections along the way. Embrace the journey, trust yourself, and always stand up for what you need. You deserve a life that truly reflects your dreams, and it all starts with the courage to ask for it.

"*If a girl wants to be a legend, she should go ahead and be one.*"

— Calamity Jane

STOP OVERANALYZING

Have you ever spent hours replaying a conversation in your head over and over again? You agonize over the other person's phrases, body language, and tone, trying to uncover the "real truth." Then, because you need perspective, you call several friends and rehash the whole thing, play by play, to see what they think the hidden meaning is. If this is you, you're overanalyzing.

While not every girl overanalyzes, many of us do, especially in our younger years. We spend significant time worrying about how we are coming across, how our shoes look with our outfit, how our hair looks, if this or that person likes us, what other people think of us, and... it goes on and on. As you get older, you realize that most of this overanalyzing is a reflection of our lack of confidence and insecurity, not to mention a giant waste of energy.

While not every man takes things at face value, many of them do. Where it gets sticky for many of us women is in the workplace, where men represent the majority. When a man says "I don't want to talk about it anymore," that's exactly what they mean. However, if a woman says this, it frequently means the opposite. Women who can let things roll off their back and avoid the overanalyzing rabbit hole are able to reserve their energy for more important conversations. As a result, they're also taken more seriously when they speak.

Understanding Why You May Be Overanalyzing

Why might you be trapped in the overanalyzing cycle? There are a number of potential contributing factors:

You're super empathetic. Many women are raised to be nurturing, always paying attention to how others feel. This can lead to overthinking every interaction, trying to figure out what everyone else is feeling or thinking.

Society's expectations are heavy. There's often

pressure to meet certain standards—whether it's in how you look, your career, or your relationships. This pressure can make you scrutinize every decision, wondering if you're doing it "right."

Stress is taking over. When you're juggling a lot, it's natural to start overanalyzing everything, trying to anticipate problems before they happen. The stress of balancing multiple roles can make this even worse.

Perfectionism is creeping in. Maybe you feel like you have to be perfect in everything you do, and social media doesn't help. This drive for perfection can cause you to overthink decisions to avoid any mistakes.

Self-esteem is a struggle. If you're feeling low about yourself, it's easy to get stuck on your flaws or mistakes, going over them again and again in your mind.

Anxiety and depression are real. These mental health challenges often bring intrusive thoughts that won't quit. You might find yourself stuck in a loop of worries or sadness.

Trauma sticks with you. If you've been through

something really tough, your mind might keep replaying it, trying to make sense of what happened or figuring out how to avoid it in the future.

Unresolved issues linger. If there's something in your life that hasn't been dealt with, your brain might keep coming back to it, trying to solve the problem or understand what went wrong.

Brain chemistry plays a role. Sometimes, it's about the chemicals in your brain. Imbalances in things like serotonin can mess with your mood and make negative thoughts more persistent.

Loneliness feeds it. When you feel isolated or surrounded by negativity, it's easy to get stuck in your head. Without someone to talk to or a positive environment, those negative thoughts can take over.

The Signs Of Overanalyzing

Sometimes, when you're deep in thought, it's hard to realize you're overthinking everything. You might not even know you're doing it. Here are some signs that you could be stuck in overanalyzing mode:

Replaying every interaction: If you're constantly going over conversations in your head, dissecting every word, tone, and gesture, you're likely looking for hidden meanings that might not even be there.

Obsessing: When one situation takes over your thoughts, making it hard to enjoy time with friends or focus on anything else, it's a clear sign you're stuck in overanalyzing mode.

Constantly seeking reassurance: If you're always asking others to validate your feelings or interpretations, it shows that you're unsure and overthinking the situation.

Jumping to conclusions: Making assumptions based on limited information instead of asking for clarity is a common sign of overanalyzing.

Strong emotional reactions: If you're feeling intense emotions like anxiety, frustration, or anger over something that might not warrant it, overanalyzing could be at play.

Physical stress symptoms: Tension headaches, an

upset stomach, or difficulty sleeping can all be physical signs that your mind is in overdrive.

Second-guessing everything: Constantly doubting your decisions and judgments is a classic sign of overanalyzing.

Being extra sensitive to criticism: If any feedback feels like a personal attack, it might be because you're already overanalyzing the situation.

Break The Overanalyzing Cycle

Once you're aware that you are in the overanalyzing trap, it's time to begin developing skills to break the cycle. This requires you to be in tune with what you are thinking all the time until you have retrained yourself.

Your brain is like a movie screen. What you play on your screen will influence how you think, what you believe, and the way you act, so get in control of the playlist.

Challenge negative thoughts. Challenge negative thoughts and assumptions by questioning their validity and considering alternative perspectives. Ask yourself if there is any evidence to support your interpretations, and whether there might be other explanations for the situation. Basically, what are the facts? Just the facts. Write them down to bring things into focus and help you recognize if you are embellishing the situation.

Set time limits. Set limits on how much time you allow yourself to ruminate on a situation. Designate a specific period each day for reflecting on the situation, and then make a conscious effort to redirect your thoughts to other activities or interests. For example, I will allow myself to think nonstop about X, without any judgment, from 8 a.m. until 9 a.m. daily.

Get a therapist. Save your friends and family, and go talk to a therapist. Getting perspective from people who aren't biased toward you can help you gain insight into the situation and challenge any distorted thinking patterns.

Be kind to yourself. Be kind and compassionate toward yourself, recognizing that it's normal to sometimes struggle with overanalyzing situations. Treat yourself with the same empathy and understanding you would offer to a friend in a similar situation. If you wouldn't say it to a friend, don't say it to yourself.

Do something different. Rewire your brain by engaging in activities that distract your mind and help you focus on something other than the situation you're overanalyzing. This could include hobbies like gardening or reading, exercise like going for walks with your dog or taking golf lessons, or immersing yourself in a creative project like writing or painting. Physical exercise—not Netflix—is your friend.

Accept uncertainty. Set realistic expectations for yourself and the situation, recognizing that not everything needs to be analyzed, understood, or solved immediately. Accept uncertainty and ambiguity as natural parts of life and know that you are not in control of everything. Let it go.

Relax. Incorporate relaxation techniques into your daily routine to help manage stress and anxiety. This could include yoga, meditation, progressive muscle relaxation, or guided imagery.

Care less. Challenge perfectionistic tendencies and the need to control every aspect of a situation. Accept that mistakes and imperfections are normal parts of life, and focus on progress rather than perfection.

Focus on problem-solving. Instead of dwelling on the problem, focus on practical steps you can take to address it. Break the situation down into smaller, manageable tasks, and take action to address each one. If you're in a situation that you have no control over, move on. You don't want to waste your time thinking about something you cannot control.

Have Tough Conversations

One of the biggest causes of overanalyzing is having an unresolved issue—whether it's with a friend, family member, coworker, or even your boss. When conflict isn't dealt with, it festers and starts to spread like a weed. It begins to show up in other parts of your life. Sometimes, the only way to fix it is to go to the root of the problem and have the difficult conversation. Focus on the fact that most people don't have evil ulterior motives for your life and are just doing their best to get by. Still, taking on a difficult conversation isn't easy so here are some tips to get you started:

Time it right. Wait until you have calmed down. I know myself, and, I recognize that when I jump to conclusions, I am at risk of being too direct. If you are like me, wait 24 hours. If you are still bothered by the "thing," move forward with a one-on-one conversation. Often after you have slept on it and had a chance to calm down, you will find that either you don't care that much anymore and are comfortable letting it go or you are in a much better emotional state to deal with it.

Keep it classy. Whenever possible, aim to have what I call "clarifying conversations" in private. Your gut feeling may be spot on—after all, women are often highly skilled at reading between the lines—but it is important to create an environment where the other person feels safe to communicate without the fear of looking dumb or being embarrassed in front of colleagues or the boss. Taking the conversation "offline" ensures a more open and successful exchange.

Start on the right foot. It's important to be as anti-inflammatory as possible when signaling to the other person that you would like to have a clarifying conversation. Avoid saying things that put the other person into defense mode.

- **Don't say:** *"I've got some questions about the way you responded to my comment during the meeting."*
- **Do say:** *"When you have a moment, do you have time to meet with me? I have a question about today's meeting."*

- **Don't say:** *"We need to talk. I didn't like how you spoke to me during our last conversation."*
- **Do say:** *"I'd like to talk with you some more about how our last conversation went."*

Avoid the drama. Bring only the facts to the situation. Consider yourself a crime scene detective and you are giving a step-by-step playback of the situation. It might go something like this: *"During the meeting, when I said, 'I think we should extend the deadline,' I noticed that you tilted your head a certain way and looked at the boss. I interpreted that to mean you disagreed with me. Did I read that right?"*

Be clear with your intentions. Knowing your goal beforehand can help you keep the conversation moving in the right direction and avoid getting caught in the weeds. Think of the ideal outcome for the conversation, and use that as a guidepost to keep the conversation on track.

Accept the answer even if you don't like it. If you ask the person to explain what they meant by something, accept their answer and let it go. There is rarely a need to beat the topic to death. If they say they are sorry, accept it and move on. If they deny it, accept it and move on. You've done your part by raising awareness of the issue, so now the other person is more likely to be mindful of their behavior and words around you, knowing you're ready to hold them accountable.

Navigate the aftermath. Sometimes, being upfront with people can shake things up, and it's important to know that it might change how they see you. When you stand up for yourself or call someone out, they might feel awkward or embarrassed, and that could make things a bit tense between you. You might not be part of their inner circle anymore. You'll survive. You've got your real friends who have your back and will support you through thick and thin. Focus on those genuine connections and let the rest slide.

The Bottom Line

Overanalyzing every little detail of something can really weigh you down and keep you from fully enjoying life. When you're stuck in the cycle of overthinking, you pile on unnecessary stress and anxiety, making it tough to be present in the moment. By stepping back from constant second-guessing, you lighten your mental load and start making decisions with more confidence. This shift not only eases your mind—It also improves your relationships because you're less likely to misread people's words or actions. You'll start to trust your own judgments and abilities more, and find greater joy in everyday moments you might have otherwise missed.

"Pour yourself a drink, put on some lipstick, and pull yourself together."

— Elizabeth Taylor

SHARE YOUR OPINIONS

One of the worst things you can do as a girl is keep your opinions to yourself. However, many women feel awkward, uncomfortable, and even fearful of sharing their opinions in a boardroom or professional meeting. As with most "traditional girl rules," sharing your opinion can feel daunting and unnatural. That's because the norm for many generations has been for girls to be pretty and remain quiet, and many girls have been met with harsh consequences if they got out of their lane.

As women, we haven't had much time to learn when and how to express opinions. Voting, an activity that seems commonplace now, was not possible for women in the U.S.

until 1920, more than 130 years after men voted in the first U.S. federal election. Women have not been seen as the thought leaders men have been seen as—especially in the workplace and we are still working to overcome that. Turning points like WWII in the 1940s, when many women entered the workforce, and the Civil Rights Act of 1964 prohibited employment discrimination based on sex. This backing provided women with more confidence to assert their rights and opinions without facing legal repercussions.

Let's face it, speaking up to share your opinion can be nerve-racking. Your heart may start to race, you may lose your words, your mouth may become dry, or you might start sweating. Don't worry. These reactions are normal, and you have to push through to get to the other side. Here are a few more serious fears that may prevent you from sharing your opinion:

Saying something controversial or unpopular: You might worry that your opinion will clash with the group and cause tension. This fear is common, especially when everyone seems to agree on something. It can be intimidating to voice a different perspective, even when you know it's important.

Receiving backlash: The thought of negative reactions —criticism, anger, rejection—can be paralyzing. You might picture worst-case scenarios where your opinion is met with harsh feedback, making you hesitant to speak up at all.

Starting an argument: You might worry that sharing your thoughts could spark a heated debate. If you're someone who values peace and harmony, the idea of causing conflict might keep you silent, even if you have something valuable to say.

Being judged: You might be afraid of what others will think if you express your thoughts. This fear often comes from wanting to be liked and accepted, and worrying that people will see you differently if they disagree with you.

Facing retaliation: Maybe you're in an environment where speaking up could lead to negative consequence like a demotion, job loss, or social backlash.

Feeling like it won't matter: You might think that your opinion won't make a difference, so why bother? This feeling of futility can be discouraging, especially in places where you've seen decisions being made without considering diverse viewpoints.

Feeling under-qualified: You might worry that you don't know enough about a topic to contribute meaningfully. This can be especially true in discussions where others seem more experienced, making you question the value of your own perspective.

Women have a seat at the table now because of the brave women who came before us to pave the way. When you are hesitant to share your opinion, take a moment to think of the power that all the women before you have fought for and passed on to you. This is where you should draw your strength so you can push past all the reasons that might be holding you back from sharing your opinion. Realizing you are not alone, and that you have the strength of all the women who came before you, will help you gain the courage to speak up.

You might feel that what you have to say is not important or not going to change anything. I'm here to tell you that you matter.

Your opinions matter, and when you share them, you are not only advocating for yourself but for all the women coming up the ranks behind you.

When you don't speak up, people assume that you don't care, that you are bored with the discussion, or that you don't have thoughts on the issue.

There are many benefits to sharing your opinion, especially when you want to advance your career. When it comes time for the boss to promote someone to a leadership position, they are going to look for someone who can speak up in the room, even if you speak up just to echo something another person has said.

When you are able to effectively share your opinions, you will get noticed and earn the respect of others.

When To Share Your Opinions

There is a time and place for everything so knowing when it makes sense to speak up can put you in a power position. Here are some key moments when you should share your opinion:

To move the conversation forward: When collaborating on projects or making strategic decisions, if you have a different perspective or more insight to add to the conversation, your input can contribute to the team's success.

When you disagree: When conflicts arise, sharing your opinion respectfully can help you identify underlying issues and work toward resolution.

When someone is being treated unfairly: Speaking up about social injustices or advocating for causes you believe in can drive positive change and promote equality.

When you share your thoughts during these kinds of workplace scenarios, you'll find that people will begin to value your opinion and include you in more discussions. Quiet, shy individuals who never speak up often miss out on important conversations and meetings. Once you build a reputation for sharing your opinion, you will be viewed as a valuable contributor.

When To Keep Your Opinions To Yourself

Just as there are times to share, there are times to keep your mouth shut. Here are a few examples when sharing your opinion can quickly get you into hot water:

When it's unsolicited: If your opinion is not requested or relevant to the conversation, it may be perceived as intrusive or unnecessary.

When it's a private matter: Avoid sharing opinions on sensitive topics, such as someone's appearance, personal beliefs, or private matters, unless you're invited to do so, and in that case, do it in a respectful manner.

In the heat of the moment: In emotionally charged situations, sharing your opinion impulsively may escalate tensions or hinder productive communication. It's often better to wait until emotions have cooled before expressing your viewpoint.

When you have no idea: If you lack knowledge or expertise on a particular subject, it's advisable to refrain from offering opinions that could mislead or misinform others.

When it's rude: Refrain from expressing opinions that could harm or offend others, such as discriminatory, derogatory, or hurtful remarks. Respect diversity and cultivate empathy in your interactions with others.

When you could be in physical danger: If you are in a hostile or volatile situation, it's better to do whatever necessary to protect yourself and get to safety.

How To Share Your Opinions

Sharing your opinions can be a challenge, but with a few practical strategies, you can make your voice heard confidently and clearly. Whether you're speaking up in a meeting or joining a discussion, having a game plan can make all the difference. Here are some tried-and-true tips to help you express your thoughts effectively:

Jot down your thoughts before you speak. A few bullet points will usually do the trick so you don't forget anything.

Take three deep breaths right before you speak. This can help to lower your heart rate.

Adopt the professor pose right before you speak.

Place your thumb under your chin and index finger under your nose. Press deep into the area under your nose, above your lip. This is a pressure point that will lower your heart rate while giving the impression that you are deep in thought.

Maintain good posture and eye contact with the people in the room.

Have an opening line to get started. An example would be, *"I have a thought on this I'd like to share with the group."*

Speak slowly. Often when people are nervous they speak too fast, making it difficult to understand what they are saying.

Be concise. If people like what you're saying, they'll ask for more, giving you an opportunity to elaborate.

End with a question, like, *"Am I way off here, or does anyone agree with me?"* Then, either way, you have spoken your mind and can now have a seat.

The Benefits Of Sharing Your Opinions

Once you begin sharing your opinions regularly, you'll notice several changes begin to happen. One of the most common changes is that other people—usually women who are still uncomfortable sharing their opinions—will thank you for speaking up. They'll let you know that they felt the exact same way and were glad you said something. You might wonder why they didn't say anything or echo in agreement with you during the meeting, but understand that they are still trying to figure out how to share their opinion. Do what you can to encourage them to share their thoughts at the next meeting. It's called women empowerment and we have to help each other as much as possible.

You have a unique perspective, different from anyone else's in the world, which means your opinion matters just as much as anyone else's opinion.

Some other wins you'll experience when you start sharing your opinions include:

You'll become an influencer. As an opinion leader, you have the ability to influence decision-making and drive change within your company or community. Your insights and expertise will start to carry weight and can impact the direction of discussions and initiatives.

Doors will open. You may be approached for collaboration opportunities with others in your organization seeking your expertise. Collaborative projects can lead to new ventures, opportunities, and partnerships.

You will earn more money. Opinion leaders often have the power to command a higher salary as they are seen as valuable contributors to the company.

You'll inspire other women (and men). Sharing your perspective and ideas will inspire other people to do the same. Especially if you can help bring them along by including them in conversations until they feel more confident to speak up regularly.

You will be more confident. Being recognized as an opinion leader can be personally fulfilling, as it validates your expertise, contributions, and impact within your professional community. Knowing that your insights and efforts are valued by others can bring a sense of satisfaction and pride.

The Bottom Line

People won't always see things the same way you do. The point of sharing is to show there are other equal but different ways of seeing things that deserve consideration. The more you share your opinion, the more comfortable you will become with it yourself. You'll also appear more open and approachable to others, which in itself is a valuable skill. Sharing your opinion is a privilege that women before you have worked hard to earn, so don't sit quietly on the sidelines and let your opportunity slip away. Brush the fears aside and take a chance on yourself.

"Women have been trained to speak softly and carry a lipstick. Those days are over."

— Bella Abzug

KNOW WHEN TO APOLOGIZE

Men and women apologize at similar rates, but, compared to men, women have a lower threshold for what constitutes an offense.[1] When you think about all the things you might apologize for during a regular day, you might find that you are overdoing it when compared to your male counterparts.

Recognize When You Are Apologizing Too Much

If any of the following sound familiar, you might be unnecessarily apologizing:

- You aren't ready to order when the waiter comes to the table. *"I'm not ready yet. I'm so sorry!"*

- You have a question at work. *"I'm sorry to bother you. Can I quickly ask you a question?"*
- You have a comment in a meeting. *"I'm sorry. I don't understand how to do this task."*
- Someone gives you a funny look to suggest you might be doing something wrong, but you have no idea what that is. *"I'm sorry?"*
- You need to reach for something on the grocery store shelf and someone is standing in the way talking on the phone. *"I'm sorry. I just need to grab something off this shelf."*
- You're going on vacation and won't be able to attend a meeting. *"I'm sorry. I can't make that meeting."*

Many girls and women apologize so much that it eventually becomes a subconscious habit. Consistently over-apologizing is called the "Sorry Syndrome." Here are some things that women commonly consider an offense, and therefore they apologize for, that most men do not:

- Situations that are out of your control (like when someone is sick)
- Someone else's actions (like when someone runs into your heel with the grocery cart)
- Normal, everyday interactions (like asking a question)

- Inanimate objects (like when Siri doesn't understand your request)
- When you're trying to be assertive and are feeling uncomfortable (like in a boardroom and you can't get a word in edgewise)

When you apologize too frequently for mistakes you didn't make, you give off a vibe that you are weak, timid, insecure, and possibly defensive. You're telling yourself that you aren't as valuable as someone else, and you're telling the world that you don't feel worthy of respect.

How To Break The Over-Apologizing Cycle

The good news is that with a few tweaks, you can ditch the over-apologizing habit and still communicate with empathy. By increasing your awareness and choosing your words more thoughtfully, you can express yourself clearly and kindly without constantly saying sorry.

Be aware. Try to recognize when you say the words "I'm sorry." Then, ask yourself if you really committed an offense. If the answer is no, make a mental note of your behavior and try to avoid saying "I'm sorry" next time. You may have been apologizing for so long that it has turned in to a habit and will require some effort to stop.

Understand why. Take the time to understand the feelings and emotions that could be driving your apology when you haven't committed an offense. One of the following is likely at play:

- You feel bad for someone else.
- You wish things were different.
- You don't want to be a bother.
- You don't feel worthy.
- You use it as a filler word.

Choose new words. Start conveying the same sentiments, but leave the apology out. Here are some examples:

Old you: *"I'm so sorry. I need to grab some milk out of the refrigerator."*
New you: *"Excuse me, could I squeeze past you? I need to grab some milk out of the refrigerator."*

Old you: *"I'm sorry you don't feel well."*

New you: *"I'm sad you don't feel well."*

Old you: *"I'm sorry, but I can't make that meeting next week."*

New you: *"Is there another time we could meet? Next week doesn't work for me."*

Old you: *"I'm sorry to bother you. Can I ask a question?"*

New you: *"I have a question. Is this a good time to ask?"*

Once you get the hang of it, it will become second nature.

When you stop over-apologizing, you will experience a higher level of confidence.

How To Apologize Properly

Now, let's talk about when you should apologize and how to do it effectively without beating yourself up.

Everyone makes mistakes—usually multiple times per day. Here are some situations when you need to put your big-girl pants on and take responsibility with an apology:

- You have hurt someone's feelings.
- You have been rude.
- You have made a mistake.
- You regret something you did.
- You need to bury the hatchet and be the bigger person.

You aren't perfect. You will make mistakes like everyone else.

It isn't always easy to deliver a sincere apology. And, unless you have done something horrible, it's best to limit yourself to two apologies per offense. More than that can come across as excessive and unnecessary, except in really significant situations. Here's a simple seven-step plan for how to apologize effectively:

1. Own it. The first step to delivering a successful apology is to accept full responsibility for your actions.

2. Don't try to justify it. When you try to explain all

the reasons you did what you did, you are basically saying it wasn't your fault when in reality it was your fault.

3. Say the words with sincerity. Look the person straight in the eye and say, *"I'm sorry."*

4. Clearly state what you are sorry for. Don't try to dress it up with fancy words. Instead, be direct and say something like, *"I'm sorry I spaced our meeting and wasted your time."*

5. Wait for the other person to accept your apology. The other person's acceptance of your apology may take some time depending on the magnitude of your mistake. Be patient and allow space for the other person to think about your apology and hopefully accept it. Most mistakes, like missing a meeting, will be forgiven instantly. Others, like talking about someone behind their back, may take a little longer.

6. Say you're sorry one more time. After someone accepts your apology, say it only once more to reinforce your sentiment. *"Again, I'm sorry. Thank you for forgiving me."*

7. Forgive yourself and move on. Everyone makes mistakes. Understand that you are normal, so be kind to yourself and do your best to let it go.

So, what if you really mess up? You will undoubtedly make some big mistakes in your life—the kind of mistakes that an apology just can't fix. You must learn to forgive yourself. This is a critical part of apologizing. You might need help figuring out how to do this, so take the steps necessary to love yourself again.

The only true mistakes you make are those from which you learn nothing.

The Bottom Line

While apologizing is a sign of empathy and humility, overdoing it can actually send the wrong message—both to others and yourself. By recognizing when you're apologizing too much and consciously choosing more assertive language, you empower yourself and build confidence. Mistakes will happen, and when they do, offer a sincere apology, take responsibility, and then let it go. Don't dwell on it or beat yourself up—everyone makes mistakes, and what matters most is learning from them and moving forward. Remember, your voice matters, and you don't need to apologize for taking up space.

"Happiness and confidence are the prettiest things you can wear."

— Taylor Swift

THE "WHY NOT ME" MINDSET

I n a world filled with uncertainties and challenges, there's one powerful mindset that stands out as a beacon of hope for aspiring women: the "why not me?" mindset. This mindset is not just about self-confidence; it's a philosophy that propels individuals to believe that they are not only good enough but capable of achieving extraordinary feats.

If you only remember one part of the this book, remember this:

> **You are good enough**. The first step in adopting the "why not me?" mindset is acknowledging your own worth. You are good enough, and your unique qualities and perspectives are valuable. Understand that success often starts with self-belief. When you

truly believe in your capabilities, you become unstoppable.

You can do this. The journey of life is paved with challenges, but the "why not me?" mindset encourages you to embrace these challenges as opportunities for growth. Instead of questioning whether you can do it, ask yourself why you can't. The belief in your ability to overcome obstacles is a crucial driver of success.

People are just people. Regardless of titles and positions, people are just people. The "why not me?" mindset reminds us that everyone, no matter their status, started somewhere. Networking and building connections become easier when you approach others as equals. People relate to authenticity, and authenticity breeds success.

It's not about being the smartest. Success isn't just about having the most brains in the room. What really matters is, "Who else cares about this as much as I do?" Being truly committed to your goals, passion, and dedication can set you apart and help you achieve more than those who might know more but don't have your fire.

You've got the smarts, creativity, and resilience to succeed. It's time to tap into what's already within you.

The Bottom Line

Dig deep and unlock that inner strength you've always had. It's time to shake off the old "girl rules" that have been holding you back and replace them with beliefs that empower you. Recognize your worth and believe in your potential. Stand up for yourself and embrace your power. The world needs everything you've got.

"It's hard to be a diamond in a rhinestone world."

— Dolly Parton

REFERENCES

Ask For What You Want

1. Canfield, J., & Switzer, J. (2005). *The Success Principles: How to Get from Where You Are to Where You Want to Be.* HarperCollins.
2. Burnett, B., & Evans, D. (2016). *Designing Your Life: How to Build a Well-Lived, Joyful Life.* Knopf.
3. Meyer, P. J. (2003). *Attitude Is Everything: If You Want to Succeed Above and Beyond.* The Success Motivation Institute.

Know When To Apologize

1. Schumann, K. and Ross, M., 2010. Why women apologize more than men: Gender differences in thresholds for perceiving offensive behavior. *Psychological Science, 21*(11), pp.1649-1655.

ABOUT THE AUTHOR

Dr. Stacee Santi Longfellow, a veterinarian and entrepreneur, founded Vet2Pet, a tech platform for veterinary practices that she successfully sold in 2022. Now, she mentors female founders and young women through writing and speaking, helping them unlock their strengths and pursue their dreams with her straight-talk style and genuine authenticity.

Stacee lives in Durango, Colorado, with six horses, three dogs, one cat, three chickens, one husband and hopefully a baby burro someday.

This is her debut book.

Follow on Instagram @dr_stacee_santi
Share a note with Stacee by scanning the QR code:

Made in the USA
Monee, IL
14 January 2025